TEN TS

Top Reptiles

Lizards form the largest group of reptiles—there are nearly 4,000 different species known. They are found in more places than any other type of reptile, and live everywhere, from deserts to the Arctic tundra, and exposed mountain slopes to isolated islands. A lizard's habitat can be anything from the highest branches in a forest's trees to the soil underneath its leaf litter. Like all living reptiles, lizards are cold-blooded, which means that their body temperature varies with that of their surroundings. Most are small and feed on insects, but some have become large, dangerous carnivores. A few eat only plants. Lizards are very varied in shape and color. Most have four legs, but some have lost their legs and look like snakes.

▲ FIVE TOES, FOUR LEGS
This green lizard is a typical lizard. It is active by day and has four legs, each with five toes. Most lizards are fairly small; in the food chain, they sit between insects and the predatory birds, mammals, and snakes.

▼ LIZARD EGGS
Reptiles lay their eggs on land. Their eggs are cleidoic, which means "closed-box"—the baby develops inside the egg, isolated from the outside world and often protected by a tough, leathery shell. Nutrition is supplied by the yolk sac, and waste products are stored in a membrane called the allantois. The amnion, a protective, fluid-filled membrane, surrounds the growing baby lizard and the yolk sac.

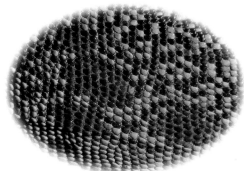

▲ SCALY SKIN
Lizards are covered in scales made of a substance called keratin, which is also the basis of human hair. Lizard scales vary in size, from the tiny grainlike scales on geckos to the large, fingernail-like scales, or scutes, of plated lizards. Scales offer protection from injury and against drying out.

MEGA MONITORS ▶

Lizards first appeared 100–150 million years ago. *Megalania priscus* was a giant Australian monitor lizard that would have made a Komodo dragon, the world's largest living lizard, look very puny. Adults reached 23 ft and may have weighed more than half a ton. They probably ate prehistoric kangaroos and giant wombats. *Megalania* lived until 25,000 years ago, and they may have met Australia's first humans.

23 ft

Megalania priscus

6 ft

10 ft

Man

Komodo dragon

◀ GIANT DRAGONS

The heaviest lizard in the world is the Komodo dragon from the group of islands of the same name in Indonesia. Although there are stories of 16½-ft-long Komodo dragons, the longest specimen ever accurately measured was 10 ft. It can weigh up to 155 lbs. The Salvador's monitor lizard from New Guinea, a more slimline and lighter relative, may grow longer, to over 13 ft.

MINI MARVELS ▶

The Nosy Be pigmy chameleon from Northern Madagascar grows to no more than 1½ in long, but it is not the smallest living lizard. Even smaller is the Jaragua gecko from the Dominican Republic in the Caribbean. It grows to a maximum length of just ½ in and was discovered in 2001. It is the world's smallest lizard and the smallest land-living vertebrate (animal with a backbone) known to science.

5

Lizard Relatives

▲ RELATION WITH A SHELL
Turtles and tortoises belong to an ancient order of reptiles that split from the main reptile line shortly after the ancestors of mammals did. They are distantly related to other modern reptiles—in fact, lizards are related less to turtles and tortoises than they are to dinosaurs or birds. Turtles live in the sea and fresh water, while tortoises live on land.

▲ DINOSAUR DINNER
In this reconstruction, a plant-eating *Iguanodon* is being stalked by two meat-eating *Deinonychus*. Although dinosaurs might look like giant lizards they were more closely related to crocodiles and birds. Unlike modern reptiles, many dinosaurs walked on two legs. Most of these ancient reptiles were plant-eaters but some ate meat.

The first reptiles appeared on Earth over 260 million years ago. Most types that lived in the distant past, such as dinosaurs and flying pterodactyls, are extinct today. Even so the Class Reptilia currently contains over 7,000 living species, ranging from turtles to crocodiles and geckos to snakes. All reptiles have scaly or leathery protective skin, which allows them to survive in salty, hot or dry conditions that would kill many other animals. Most lay leathery-shelled eggs, but a few lizards and snakes bear live young —an adaptation to living in colder climates where eggs would die. This versatility makes reptiles excellent survivors. Even though we now live in the Age of Mammals, reptiles are still a very successful group.

▲ FIERCE HUNTER
Crocodiles and alligators include the largest reptiles alive today. Nile crocodiles such as this can grow to 20 ft long and weigh almost a ton, and the Indo-Pacific crocodile is even larger. Crocodilians eat meat and spend most of their time in water. They are distantly related to lizards and, like all egg-laying reptiles, they lay eggs on land.

Congo Monster

People living in the Congo rainforest claim it is inhabited by a giant Diplodocus-*like creature that they call Mokele-mbembe. Do dinosaurs still walk the Earth or could the monster be a large monitor lizard standing on its hind feet and stretching out its long neck? Several expeditions have set out in search of Mokele-mbembe but the mystery remains unsolved.*

THE FAMILY TREE ▼

As this tree shows, reptiles are a very diverse group. Turtles split away from the main reptilian line millions of years ago. Reptiles then divided into two main groups. The Archosauria (ancient reptiles) became dinosaurs, crocodilians, and birds. The Lepidosauria (scaled reptiles) includes tuataras, and modern lizards, snakes, and amphisbaenians (worm-lizards).

▲ TWO TUATARAS

These reptiles live on islands off the coast of New Zealand. Although they look like lizards, they have their own reptile group. They have hardly changed their appearance and behavior since dinosaurs walked the Earth. Only two species of tuatara are alive in the world today.

▼ LEGLESS LIZARDS

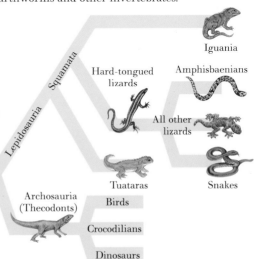

Amphisbaenians, or worm-lizards, are legless reptiles that evolved from lizards. There are around 130 species, living in Florida, northwestern Mexico, the West Indies, South America, Africa, and Mediterranean Europe. Burrowers in soil and sand, amphisbaenians feed on earthworms and other invertebrates.

Iguania

Amphisbaenians

Hard-tongued lizards

Squamata

All other lizards

Lepidosauria

Turtles and tortoises

Amphibians

Tetrapods

Tuataras

Snakes

Mammal-like reptiles

Archosauria (Thecodonts)

Birds

Mammals

Crocodilians

Dinosaurs

The Iguania

Lizards are split into two main groups. The first of these is known to scientists as the Iguania, and contains over 1,300 species, including iguanas, agamas, chameleons, anoles, swift lizards, lava lizards, basilisks, and spiny lizards. The Iguania is an ancient group of reptiles that dates back almost 100 million years. It is split into two smaller groups, because agamas and chameleons have different teeth and live on different continents to iguanas and most of their relatives. Although some agamas look like iguanas, this is because they have become alike as a result of having similar lifestyles, and not because they are closely related.

▲ AMAZING AGAMAS

There are 300 species of agama, living in southeastern Europe, Asia, Africa, and Australia. Many agamas are sun lovers, and include desert-dwellers such as the frilled lizards and this eastern bearded dragon. This family also contains the tiny flying lizards of Southeast Asia and the secretive rain forest dragons of New Guinea and Queensland in Australia.

COLOR-CHANGING CHAMELEONS ▶

This veiled chameleon comes from the Yemen, on the Arabian Peninsula. With their "turret-eyes," curly prehensile tails, famous color-changing capabilities, and long, sticky tongues, the chameleons must be the strangest family of lizards in the world. Although most of the 160 species live in Africa and Madagascar, the Indian chameleon comes from southern Asia, and the European chameleon is found in southern Spain and Crete.

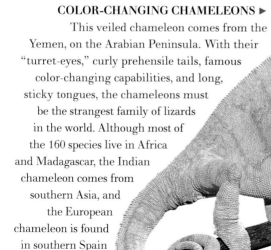

Did you know? Chameleons can change the color of their skin to match their surroundings.

8

IGUANAS AND CHUCKWALLAS ▶
Most iguanas, and their close relatives, the chuckwallas, live in the Americas. Many are found in the West Indies, including the powerful rhinoceros iguanas. The Central and South American green iguana is perhaps the most familiar lizard in the world, but not all iguanas are American. The iguana on the right is from Fiji, in the Pacific Ocean.

SWIFT SPECIES ▶
This Cuvier's Malagasy swift lives in the dry scrub and rocky outcrops of Madagascar, a large island off the eastern coast of Africa. In all, seven insect-eating species of small, tree- and rock-dwelling swifts live there. They lay four to six eggs. Another family of small fast-moving lizards known as swifts come from the Americas, from the USA down to Argentina.

▲ NATIVE KNIGHTS
The knight anole is a native of Cuba, but it was introduced to southern Florida in 1952. There it hunts down the smaller green anole, which has become an endangered species in Florida, although it lives in many other parts of the world, including Hawaii. There are about 400 species of anoles in South America and the West Indies.

DASHING BASILISKS ▶
The plumed basilisk is the largest species of basilisk. The four species, together with the helmeted and cone-headed lizards, make up a small, rain forest-dwelling family that comes from Central America and northern South America. They are sometimes called "Jesus lizards", because they can dash across water for some distance before breaking the surface.

OUT OF AFRICA

Jackson's three-horned chameleon inhabits woodland on the slopes of Africa's Mount Kenya, but can also be found in the suburbs of Kenya's capital city, Nairobi. Males have longer horns than females. Small populations have become established on the Hawaiian Islands after pet Jackson's chameleons were released.

Focus on

When most people think of a chameleon, they imagine a big, color-changing lizard with horns. This "typical chameleon" image does not do justice to this diverse family of lizards. Most of the 160 or so species are split fifty-fifty between Africa and Madagascar, but there is also a species in southern Europe, one on the Arabian Peninsula and another in India. Not all chameleons live in rain forests—many inhabit dry woodland and some are found in deserts. The idea of chameleons being green lizards that can change color is also a generalization—some of the smaller species are brown and they cannot change their color at all.

GIANT OF THE FORESTS

Parson's chameleon can reach 27 in long. This giant from Madagascar is the second-largest chameleon, after Oustalet's chameleon, which also comes from Madagascar. Parson's chameleon is an inhabitant of the island's wet eastern forest, and it rarely changes color.

EASTERN COLOR

The South Asian chameleon, or Indian chameleon, is found from Pakistan and India to northern parts of Sri Lanka. The only truly Asian chameleon, it lives in dry forests and woodland. It lays up to 30 eggs in early winter. Although winter might seem a strange time to lay eggs, this is actually the dry season where this chameleon lives.

Chameleons

FIT TO DROP

Its short tail, brown pigmentation and dark lines make the West African leaf chameleon look like a dead leaf hanging from a twig. It does not change color. If it is disturbed, it just falls to the ground and lies still, blending in with the dead brown leaves on the forest floor. This small lizard reaches maturity in three months, and it feeds on termites, which it finds on the short, rain forest shrubs where it lives.

DESERT DWELLER

Chameleons are usually associated with rain forest and woodland, but some species live in the desert. The Namaqua chameleon is found in the arid regions of Namibia and western South Africa. It spends most of its time on the ground, but will climb up on rocks and into bushes to keep cool. The Namaqua chameleon has a large mouth and eats all kinds of animals, from insects to small lizards and snakes.

FAST DEVELOPERS

Natal dwarf chameleons live in dry thickets and gardens in South Africa. Males vary in color and may be bright blue or red. Females and juveniles are gray, brown, or green. The Natal chameleon gives birth to between eight and twenty live babies. These youngsters grow fast and can have babies of their own by the time they are nine months old. Such rapid development is a characteristic of many chameleons.

Hard Tongues

All lizards not contained in the Iguania belong to a group known as the Scleroglossa, or hard-tongued lizards. Their tongues are tough and flat. There are more than 2,700 species of hard-tongued lizard, ranging in size from the tiny insectivorous Caribbean least geckos to large carnivorous monitor lizards. Many of the 17 families have become burrowers and have lost their legs, after millions of years of them getting smaller and smaller to make burrowing easier. Hard-tongued lizards are the ancestors of amphisbaenians and snakes. They include a huge variety of species, among them geckos, lacertid lizards, zonures, skinks, anguid lizards, and monitor lizards.

▲ STICKY FINGERS

Most geckos are nocturnal and hunt insects. The larger species, such as this tokay gecko, include other lizards in their diet. Geckos are well known for their ability to walk up walls and tree trunks, and across ceilings. They do this with the help of flattened toes that have special plates called scansors underneath. Not all geckos can climb like this, however.

SUN LOVERS ►

Europe's eyed lizard preys on many smaller lizards, insects, and spiders. Like most of the lizards that are commonly seen in Europe, it belongs to the lacertid family. Indeed the green lizards, wall lizards, and ruin lizards often seen basking in the sun are all lacertids. The most widespread European species is the viviparous lizard. Other lacertids live in Africa and Asia. All lacertids are active and alert hunters of insects and spiders.

◄ REAR GUARD

The sungazer is the largest of the zonures, which are also called girdled lizards because their spiny scales are arranged in rings, or girdles, around the body. The sungazer has extremely spiny scales on its tail. The scales are used to defend the lizard when it dives headfirst down a hole or wedges itself into a rocky crevice.

SMOOTHLY DOES IT ►

Most skinks, including this Müller's skink, have smooth shiny scales. Skinks make up the largest lizard family. Most skinks are small, active by day, live on the ground, and eat insects. However, the Solomon's monkey-tail skink breaks all the rules by being a tree-living plant-eater that is active by night.

▲ WORM, SNAKE, OR LIZARD?

The European slowworm is a legless lizard that feeds on slugs and other soft-bodied creatures. It is the best-known anguid lizard, but not all anguids lack limbs—the American alligator lizards have short legs, but they still wriggle along. The longest anguid is the 3-ft European glass lizard. It looks like a snake, but it is a true lizard with eyelids and ear openings.

▲ ALMOST INVISIBLE

This Indo-Malay water monitor is almost invisible against the rock it is lying on. Like other monitor lizards, it is a good climber and swimmer. They are found in Africa and Asia, but most live in Australia, and range in size from the 10-in-long short-tailed monitor to the giant Komodo dragon. Most eat insects or vertebrates but Gray's monitor also eats fruit.

Amphisbaenians

The amphisbaenians, also known as worm lizards, are a group of reptiles that evolved from lizards. Worm lizards have tiny eyes that are covered by transparent scales, and rely mainly on taste, smell, and hearing to find their way around. They are found in Florida, the West Indies, Mexico, South America, southern Europe, the Middle East, and Africa. Although they are widely distributed, worm lizards are not very well understood because they are rarely seen. They are secretive burrowers and resemble earthworms. Most species can discard their tails in defense, but they cannot grow new ones, unlike many true lizards. Most worm lizards lay eggs, although a few bear live young. All feed on soft-bodied invertebrates, such as worms and insect larvae (young).

▲ **WHITE GIANT**
The largest amphisbaenian is the white worm lizard of South America. It can grow to at least 22 in long and has a pointed snout and a blunt, rounded tail. It hunts deep in the nests of leaf-cutting ants. The white worm lizard follows ant trails back to the nest and enters the refuse area deep below the ants' carefully cultured fungus gardens. Once it is there, it feeds on beetle larvae.

◄ **ANT EATER**
Black and white worm lizards live in South America in the Amazon rain forest. It is a large species—like the white worm lizard—and it can reach up to 12 in long. The black and white worm-lizard's striking pattern contrasts with its light pink head, which is usually marked with a single, central black spot. This species lives in ant nests, where it lays its eggs and feeds mainly on ant larvae and pupae. It is seen above ground only after heavy rain.

WEIRD AND WONDERFUL ▼

The ajolates, or mole worm lizards, are among the strangest of all reptiles. Like other worm lizards, they have elongated bodies covered with rings of small rectangular scales. The three known species of mole worm lizards also have a pair of front feet for digging. Mole worm lizards inhabit sandy, low-lying country in Mexico. Their bodies have a long fold running from one end to the other. This fold may allow the body to expand when they feed and breathe.

Did you know? In Greek myths the amphisbaenia was a monstrous snake with a head at each end.

◄ SOLE EUROPEAN

Europe's only amphisbaenian is the Iberian worm lizard, which lives in Spain and Portugal. It has close relatives in Morocco. Usually black, brown, or yellow, with a paler underside and sometimes speckled with pink, at first sight, this species looks like an earthworm. However, a closer examination will reveal a specialized, pointed head for burrowing, a mouth with a short tongue, and tiny, faint eyes. The body is ringed with rows of tiny, square scales. Rarely seen above ground, this species is found under flat stones and in leaf litter in sandy woodland, and it feeds on a wide variety of insects.

◄ TOP TUNNELER

The checkered worm lizard inhabits open rocky country and woodland in North Africa. It has a slightly pointed head and a stout body patterned with dark brown spots on a lighter background. When it is threatened, the checkered worm lizard may roll into a ball. This species belongs to the most advanced family of worm lizards, which have developed specialized techniques for tunnel excavation.

15

Where in the World

Lizards are the most numerous of all reptiles, and they are also among the most adaptable—they live in regions where even snakes are absent. Lizards have adapted to cope with cold on mountains and inside the Arctic Circle and can endure the heat of any desert. They are excellent colonizers—especially those species that give birth to live young—and can adapt in time to feed on anything that is available. In fact, almost everywhere you look on land, there is a good chance a lizard lives there. Unlike amphibians, which lived on Earth before reptiles, some lizards have learned to live in or near the sea, and have adapted to high levels of salt in their diets.

▲ DUSTY DESERT
Many lizards live in deserts but surviving there is hard. Desert lizards are often nocturnal to avoid the heat. They rarely drink, and many survive on the water they get from their food alone. Some desert lizards, such as this Namib gecko, have webbed feet or fringes on their toes to help them run over sand.

▲ ICY COLD
The Arctic is not an ideal place for reptiles, but a few lizards do live in this cold region and are active in the short summers. The viviparous lizard is common throughout Europe, but unlike other European lizards, it is also found well inside the Arctic Circle. Viviparous means live-bearing, and most reptiles that live in cold climates give birth to live young.

▲ SEASHORE SALT
The swollen-snouted, side-blotch lizard is one of the few lizards that live on the seashore. It lives on the tiny island of Isla Coloradito, off Mexico, where it eats shore-living crustaceans called slaters and the sea lice that infest the sea lion colony. The salt level in its diet is 20 times the lethal level of other lizards. Special glands in its nostrils help it get rid of some of the salt.

◀ WHERE DO LIZARDS LIVE?

Lizards inhabit every continent apart from Antarctica, and have colonized most island groups. Some species, such as house geckos, have even used human transportation to reach and colonize islands a long way from land. Lizards are not found in areas of very high altitude and latitude, because it is too cold for them. The five species shown on these two pages are from different continents and different habitats. The only thing these lizards have in common is that they all survive in difficult conditions.

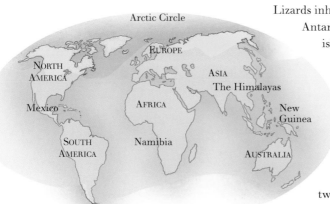

Lizards live on every continent except the Antarctic

MOUNTAIN HIGH ▶

The mountains are tough places for reptiles, which rely on the sun to keep them warm and active. Few lizards can survive in these conditions, but one exception is the rock agama from the southern Himalayas. It is found as high as 7,500 ft., basking on rocks along the freezing rivers that pour from glaciers. The rock agama hibernates in winter to save energy and avoid the worst of the cold.

◀ STEAMY RAIN FOREST

Lizards are everywhere in rain forests: in the canopy, on the tall trunks, down on the ground and underneath the leaf litter. There is plenty of food in the forest, but there are also plenty of predators, so lizards have to be alert. New Guinea's twin-crested anglehead lizard lives in rain forests, but it is seldom seen because it is well camouflaged.

17

A Marine

The marine iguana of the Galapagos Islands off Ecuador is the only truly oceangoing lizard in the world. It lives its entire life along the coast, never venturing far inland, and it survives on a diet of seaweed and the droppings of seals and crabs, which provides bacteria to aid its digestion. This diet results in dangerously high levels of salt entering the lizard's body. To avoid being poisoned, marine iguanas get rid of the salt with loud snorts, spraying the white particles of salt on the rocks, themselves, and their neighbors. A typical day for a marine iguana is spent mostly basking in the sun and feeding.

SUNBATHERS
Basking is very important to marine iguanas, especially the males, which dive into the cold waters to feed. Without basking, they would be unable to warm up enough for their bodies to digest their food. Basking marine iguanas must be alert for predators. Snakes and birds of prey will kill small iguanas if they can catch them.

UNDERWATER BREAKFAST
Female and young marine iguanas forage for food on the exposed rocks at low tide, but the adult males are more adventurous. They dive into the water and swim down to the submerged seaweed beds to browse. Large males can dive as deep as 33 ft in search of a meal.

HEAD TO HEAD
Male marine iguanas do not fight over feeding grounds, but they do disagree over mating territories. A mating territory is an area where an adult male has a good chance of meeting and courting females. These small patches of rock are disputed with body postures, head bobs, gaping mouths, and head-butting, until one male gives in and leaves.

Iguana's Day

GROUP LIVING

Marine iguanas are unusual for large lizards—
they gather together at night to sleep in groups,
like sea lions. They even manage to sleep piled
on top of each other. Marine iguanas are much
less territorial than land iguanas, so fights do
not break out over sleeping areas. By sleeping
huddled together, they conserve energy and cool
down more slowly than if they slept alone.

COURTSHIP FINERY

During the breeding season, the male marine
iguana develops large patches of red, and
sometimes green skin, which is in strong contrast
to his usual black or dark-gray color. At this
time, he is interested in mating with as many
females as possible, and spends a lot of
his time trying to fight off smaller males and
compete with larger males for mating territories.

ALL AT SEA

To get from one rocky outcrop to another, or to reach the
deeper, richer feeding grounds, the marine iguana must
venture into the sea. These lizards are extremely strong
swimmers, powered by muscular tails, and this is essential
because currents around the Galapagos are very strong.

Bone and Cartilage

backbone

rib cage

skull

The scaffolding that supports a lizard's body is called bone. This is a living tissue that develops as a lizard matures from juvenile to adult. In hatchlings, the body is supported by flexible cartilage. As a lizard ages, calcium is deposited in the cartilage and it hardens, thickens, and becomes bone. Lizards obtain calcium from their food. Different lizards have different skeletons, and scientists have divided lizards into families based mostly on skeletal features and the way bones develop.

▲ LIZARD SKELETON

Most lizards have four legs, each ending in five toes. As with all reptiles, the body is supported by the backbone, which stretches from the neck to the tail. The backbone is actually not one bone but many small bones, or vertebrae. Important organs, such as the heart and lungs, are protected by the rib cage. The skull forms a tough case around the brain.

▼ FASCINATING HORNS

Many lizards have extra structures that stick out from their body. Johnston's chameleon has three large horns on the front of its head. The horns are made of soft tissue, and they grow from raised structures on the skull. All Johnston's chameleons have these horns, but they are larger on males than females. Male use their horns to intimidate rivals, and they may also be helpful in attracting a female mate.

▲ LOST LIMBS

Some lizards have less than five toes; others have lost all their limbs. Scaly-feet lizards have completely lost their front legs, and all that remains of their hind limbs is a small scaly flap. Despite the small size of the scaly flaps, they are used for gripping and moving across rock.

monitor lizard skull

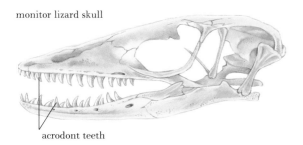

monkeytail skink skull
(*not to scale*)

acrodont teeth

pleurodont teeth

▲ SKULL AND TEETH

Monitor lizards, chameleons, iguanas, and agamas have their teeth on top of the jawbone, which is known as acrodont. Other lizards, such as the monkeytail skink, have pleurodont teeth, positioned on the side of the jawbone. The lower jawbones are linked to the back of the skull by a ball and socket joint.

Did you know? Many lizards are classified by the structure of the bones in their skull.

◄ DEFENSIVE UMBRELLA

When the Australian frilled lizard feels threatened, it opens its mouth. This action causes a wide frill of skin around its neck to open like an umbrella. The frill is supported by special bones but is poorly developed in juveniles. It is intended to frighten an enemy and give the lizard time to turn and run away. At rest, or when the lizard is running or climbing, the frill is folded along the body.

SPECIAL SAILS ►

Some lizards have a sail-like fin on their back. Supported by cartilage or bony extensions from the backbone, these fins may serve more than one purpose. In chameleons, they may aid balance or help with camouflage by making the lizard look more like a leaf. They also increase a lizard's body surface area to make it easier to warm up quickly in the sun.

Internal Anatomy

Although on the outside, lizards look much like other living creatures, under the skin all kinds of peculiar anatomical adaptations help make them successful. Lizards have special breath-holding abilities, extra sensory organs and telescopic (extendable) tongues. A few species even have green blood to protect them from parasites. Internal anatomy covers everything beneath the skin, from the skeleton and muscles to the organs and blood. It includes not only the bones, but also the muscles, tendons, and ligaments that let the skeleton move, and soft-tissue organs such as the brain, thoracic, and abdominal organs.

▲ DIVING HOUDINIS

When a green iguana that is basking over a river feels threatened, it may leap into the water, around 30 ft below, swim to the bottom, and stay there for up to 30 minutes. Iguanas can hold their breath and survive underwater like this by changing the flow of blood through the heart. Instead of sending blood from the body to the lungs, they pump it back through the body and use every bit of oxygen that is in it before they need to breathe again.

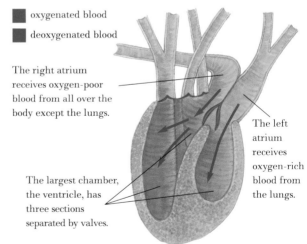

■ oxygenated blood

■ deoxygenated blood

The right atrium receives oxygen-poor blood from all over the body except the lungs.

The left atrium receives oxygen-rich blood from the lungs.

The largest chamber, the ventricle, has three sections separated by valves.

▲ THREE-CHAMBERED HEART

A lizard's heart has three chambers, unlike ours, which has four. Two chambers, called the atria, receive blood from the body. Oxygen-rich blood from the left atrium is kept separate from oxygen-poor blood from the right.

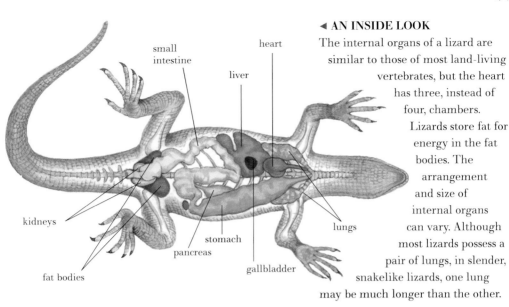

small intestine

heart

liver

kidneys

stomach

pancreas

fat bodies

gallbladder

lungs

◄ AN INSIDE LOOK

The internal organs of a lizard are similar to those of most land-living vertebrates, but the heart has three, instead of four, chambers. Lizards store fat for energy in the fat bodies. The arrangement and size of internal organs can vary. Although most lizards possess a pair of lungs, in slender, snakelike lizards, one lung may be much longer than the other.

TONGUE AND GROOVES ►

Lizards' tongues begin at the front of their mouths, as you can see in this photograph of a fat-tailed gecko's mouth. Mammals' tongues begin at the back of the throat. The open airway or glottis can be seen in the gecko's mouth. Forked-tongued lizards, such as monitors, have an extra organ, known as Jacobson's organ, which they use to analyze scent particles. The lizard places the tips of its tongue in two grooves in the roof of the mouth, which lead to the organ above.

◄ PROTECTIVE PIGMENT

Most lizards have red blood but one unusual group has blood that is green. Green-blooded skinks have a green pigment in their blood that would be poisonous to most animals. In the past it was thought that the skinks had this so that they would be unpleasant to eat. It is now believed the green pigment protects the skinks from blood parasites, such as the ones that cause malaria.

Skin and Scales

All reptiles have tough and almost completely waterproof skin. Lizard skin is made of three layers. The outer layer, or epidermis, is usually transparent and is shed regularly as the lizard grows. Under the epidermis is a layer called the stratum intermediate, which contains the pigments that give the lizard color. Beneath that is the inner layer, or dermis. In many hard-tongued lizards, this layer contains rigid plates called osteoderms ("bone skin"), which add strength to the skin. Scales vary in shape and texture from the smooth, rounded scales of skinks to the sharp, keeled (ridged) scales of zonures. Lizards don't have sweat glands as mammals do, but they have special glands between the scales.

▲ ARMOR PLATES

Plated lizards, such as this southern African, rough-scaled, plated lizard, have rectangular platelike scales arranged in regular overlapping rows around the body. These scales are strengthened by the presence of protective osteoderms (bony plates). Along each of the lizard's flanks is a long fold of skin containing small granular scales. This allows the lizard to expand its body when it breathes, in what would otherwise be a very constricting suit of armor.

SMOOTH AND SHINY ▶

This slowworm and many ground-dwelling skinks have bodies covered in small, rounded, smooth scales that give little resistance when the reptile is burrowing and moving underneath debris. The slowworm is legless so when it sheds its epidermis, the entire layer often comes off in one large piece, not inside out like a snake. The skin of the slowworm contains protective osteoderms.

▲ TINY BEADS

The Salvador's monitor lizard, which is a large, tree-climbing lizard from New Guinea, has numerous tiny scales. The smaller and more regular a lizard's scales are, the more flexible its body is. The Gila monster and beaded lizard have scales that look even more like beads.

▲ MOBILE FOLDS

The small scales of South America's northern tegu are arranged in a series of overlapping triangular folds. The northern tegu is a speedy hunter, and this arrangement of scale groups, which move over each other as the lizard runs, gives the tegu both protection and agility.

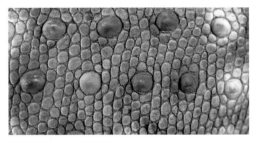

▲ SHARP RIDGES

The back of the Bosc monitor lizard from the African savannas has numerous interlocking but nonoverlapping, keeled scales. Those on the lizard's underside are smaller and not keeled. Keeled scales may help dew condense on the lizard's back at night, giving it water to drink in an otherwise arid environment.

▲ SCATTERED SCALES

Geckos have granular, velvety, or papery skin. The tokay gecko has scattered conical scales surrounded by smaller, granular scales. The skin of smaller geckos is usually much more fragile. One species from Madagascar sheds all three layers of its skin if it is grasped.

OFF WITH THE OLD ▶

Lizards must shed the outer layer of their skins in order to grow. Unlike snakes, they tend to shed their skin in pieces. This wonder gecko has begun to shed its old skin. Since the cells that produce pattern and color are in the second layer, the old skin looks colorless. The original colors are visible in the new gecko that emerges.

How Lizards

BROKEN GLASS

Many lizards can lose their tails for protection. This Australian scaly-foot has a long tail that can be quickly discarded if it is grasped. The European slowworm got its scientific name, *Anguis fragilis*, from the fact that it is "broken" easily. The scheltopusik got its other name, glass snake, because it is legless and has the habit of breaking its extremely long tail.

Small lizards often show their tails when they are threatened. Some species have bright-colored tails that, when combined with a tail-waving motion, attract a predator's attention and draw its attack away from the lizard's head and body. As a predator pounces on the lizard's tail, powerful muscular contractions in the tail make it snap off. The discarded tail thrashes around, so that the predator's attention is further distracted and the lizard can escape. The muscles at the severance point collapse and seal the tail's end to prevent blood loss. Soon the wound heals and the lizard grows a new tail.

broken tail

new tail

TAIL INTACT

The common house gecko has many enemies that would like to make a meal of it. This gecko has been lucky—it still has its original tail, but would be ready to sacrifice it in a minute if it was threatened by a predator. The original tail has a pattern like that on the body and has different scales on the top from those underneath.

THE ESCAPE MECHANISM

Lizards that can lose their tails have special breaking points built into them. When the tail is grasped, powerful muscular contractions will cause a fracture right through the tail, severing it at that point. The muscles then close the wound preventing further loss of blood.

Grow New Tails

A LOST TAIL

A lizard may try to escape being captured by losing its tail. At first, this house gecko's tail thrashes around vigorously, but it is now still and lying upside down. Since the muscle bundles in the injured base of the tail have collapsed to seal the wound, there has been little blood loss. Although the gecko may look strange without its tail, at least it is still alive and can escape from its enemy. It has survived its ordeal and can continue living. A new tail will grow to replace the one it has lost.

NEARLY AS GOOD AS NEW

This house gecko lost its tail some time ago and has now grown a new one. The new tail is supported not by bone, but by a rod of cartilage—the same material you have in the bridge of your nose. The new tail does not look as good as the old one, it looks like a cheap, extra part, but it does the job almost as well as the original.

A LIZARD WITH TWO TAILS

When a lizard loses only part of its tail, it can grow what is called a bifurcated tail. This house gecko escaped, with the original tail loosely attached to the body. Since the blood vessels survived, the original tail recovered. But another tail grew out from the open wound, resulting in a curious fork-tailed gecko.

Getting Around

The typical lizard has four well-developed legs, each with five clawed toes. The legs stick out from the side of the body. This means that the body is thrown into S-shaped curves when the lizard walks and runs. Lizard backbones are flexible to let the lizard move easily as its stride lengthens. Some lizards run very fast on all fours. Others run even faster using just their hind legs with the front of the body raised and the tail for balance. In tree-dwelling species, the feet and tail may be adapted for climbing.

▲ SPIDER MEN
Geckos are famous for their ability to run up walls and glass, but not all geckos can do this. Only the geckos with expanded digits, such as house geckos and tokay geckos, can climb sheer surfaces. Under their toes are a series of flattened plates called "scansors," which mean they can stick on to almost any flat surface.

▲ A FIFTH LIMB
Some tree-living lizards have prehensile tails, which they can use when climbing. The monkey-tail skink is a large lizard from the Solomon Islands that uses its powerful tail when clambering in the forest canopy.

▼ WALKING ON WATER
Basilisks escape predators by running very fast on their long-toed hind-limbs. They can sprint across water for quite awhile before they break the surface of the water and fall in. This unusual ability to run on water has earned them the nickname of "Jesus lizard." Some other long-legged lizards can also run on water.

▲ LEAP FOR FREEDOM

Flying lizards and flying geckos do not actually fly but glide down from trees to avoid predators. The flying gecko has webs of skin between its toes and also along the side of its body to slow its descent, but this flying lizard is more elaborate. It has a pair of "wings" spread out by false ribs to produce the lizard equivalent of a parachute.

▲ LIFE UNDERGROUND

Many desert lizards spend part of their lives underground, escaping there from enemies and the heat of the sun. Africa's sand fish disappears into loose sand extremely rapidly, digging with its legs and flattened snout. Other lizards have developed an elongated body and lost their limbs, so that they can swim through the sand like eels in water.

Night Fighters

"Gecko" is an onomatopoeic word—a word that sounds like what it describes. This comes from the Malay word "gekok," which is derived from the noise that some geckos make when they call. The tokay gecko has another call that sounds like "tow-kay." Geckos are active after dark, and this led the Japanese to give the name "Gekkoh" to their night-fighter aircraft in World War II.

HOLDING ON ▶

Chameleons' toes are fused together. Each foot has three toes opposing two toes. The toes grip in the same way as a human's opposing thumb and other four fingers. This makes the chameleon such an expert climber that it can walk along slender twigs.

29

Sensing the Surroundings

Lizards have a variety of finely tuned sense organs to allow them to move around, locate and capture prey, avoid predators, and find a mate. Eyesight is an important sense for most lizards, but the structure of the retina (the back of the inside of the eye) varies a lot. The retinas of day-living lizards are dominated by cells called cones, giving them detailed vision, and those of nocturnal species have far more light-sensing rod cells, which increases their ability to see by moonlight. Lizards that are active at dusk and dawn have vertical pupils that close down to protect the sensitive retina from bright daylight. Day-living lizards may also possess color vision.

▲ **EAGLE EYES**

Lizards that are active by day, such as the green iguana, have excellent vision. Focusing for studying close detail is accomplished by changing the shape of the soft, deformable lens of the eye. Many lizards need to be able to focus rapidly, because they move around quickly and with agility, so that they can catch fast-moving insects. Vision is also important for basking lizards, since they must be able to locate approaching predators.

◄ **LOOKING TWO WAYS AT ONCE**

Chameleons are the only land vertebrates with eyes that move independently. This Parson's chameleon can use its turret-eyes to look in two directions at the same time. When an insect is located, both eyes converge on the prey and, working like a telephoto lens, they focus quickly and precisely to enlarge the image. The turret-eyes and the long sticky tongue evolved to work together, making chameleons expert shots when they shoot out their tongues to capture insects.

▼ A THIRD EYE

Green iguanas and many other lizards have a small circular object in the middle of their heads. This is the pineal eye, a third eye with a lens, retina, and a nerve feeding back into the brain, but it has no muscles, making it unable to focus. The pineal eye may help basking lizards to monitor how much sunlight they are receiving, but the way in which it works is not yet fully understood.

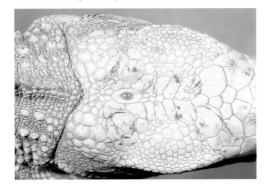

▲ LISTENING LIZARDS

Lizard ears are made up of three parts: the outer, middle, and inner ear. The eardrum of this bearded dragon is visible on the side of its head, because the outer ear is absent. In other species, the eardrum is hidden by a deep, outer ear opening. Most lizards have external ears, but some have scales over them and others have no eardrum at all.

SEEK WITH FORKED TONGUE ▶

Some hard-tongued lizards have a Jacobson's organ that allows them to "taste" the air and track prey from a long way away. The forked tongue of this water monitor lizard is picking up odor particles and delivering them to the Jacobson's organ to be analyzed. The forks of the tongue help it tell direction—if more interesting particles are on the right fork, the lizard turns right.

◀ PECULIAR TASTES

The herbivorous monkey-tail skink has a bulbous tongue with a slightly bi-lobed tip that contains many taste buds. This skink does not eat insects or meat so it does not have to track down any prey, but probably uses its sensitive tongue to discriminate between suitable and unsuitable leaves. Monkey-tail skinks are social lizards, and tongue-licking may also be a way of recognizing other members of the colony.

The Carnivores

Although the majority of lizards are either partly or totally carnivorous (meat-eating), even plant-eating lizards occasionally eat insects. Many lizards are active predators, hunting down their prey and capturing it with a lightning dash. Some meat-eating lizards take advantage of wounded, sick, dying, and dead animals for an easy meal. Animals that feed like this are called scavengers. Many lizards have a strong sense of smell and are able to locate prey that is hidden or buried. Komodo dragons are said to be able to smell prey from up to 2½ miles away. Other monitor lizards, and tegus, are experts at finding turtle and crocodile eggs, as well as the eggs of other lizards.

▲ **MANY MINI MEALS**

Ants are very small prey, but some lizards specialize in eating them. The horned lizards of North America's deserts are squat, spiny lizards that feed entirely on ants. Because ants are small, hundreds must be eaten at each meal. Fortunately for horned lizards, ants occur in large numbers and swarm together when their colony is attacked.

▲ **PINPOINT ACCURACY**

A chameleon, such as this panther chameleon, approaches its insect prey with stealth, focusing both eyes on the insect to judge how far away it is and extending its head forward as it gauges the moment to strike. Once the lizard is in position, it shoots out its long tongue rapidly and then pulls it back into its mouth with the insect stuck on the tip. Chameleons have prehensile tails, adapted for grasping, which help them grip twigs and branches when they are hunting.

Did you know? The chameleon's tongue is so long that it may be twice the length of its entire body.

▼ CRUSHING BITE

The swamp-dwelling caiman lizard from the Amazon rain forest looks a little like a crocodile. This excellent swimmer hunts aquatic snails underwater, which are crushed by flat teeth in the lizard's powerful jaws.

▲ DOWN IN ONE

Most legless lizards have tiny mouths and can only eat small prey. But Burton's snake lizard, a relative of Australia's geckos, specializes in eating skinks. Its jaws are much more flexible than those of other lizards, and its teeth curve backward, allowing it to swallow prey whole and head first in the same way a snake does.

◄ FEARLESS KILLER

Most monitor lizards are true all-around carnivores—they feed on small mammals, scavenge the carcasses of lion kills, and steal eggs from crocodile nests. Unlike most other animals, large monitors are not even afraid of snakes, and often feed on them. This Nile monitor is killing a sand snake, which is helpless against the monitor lizard's crushing jaws.

DANGEROUS PREY ►

Some lizards feed on very dangerous prey. North African desert agamas usually eat harmless insects, but sometimes they make a meal of a scorpion. To do this it must act quickly, and crush the scorpion in its powerful jaws before its tail can deliver its deadly sting.

Vegetarian Lizards

Plant-eating reptiles are rare, and only tortoises, and a few turtles and lizards, have a truly vegetarian diet. Many lizards that eat vegetation also eat insects and so are really omnivores (animals that eat plants and meat). Some lizards start life eating insects and only turn vegetarian when they become adults. Most plant-eating lizards feed on leaves, which are easy to find but hard to digest. Many leaf-eating lizards select only fresh, new shoots, which are easier to digest. Eating fruit is easier but less common in lizards, and a few species feed on seeds, flower heads, or nectar. Marine iguanas eat seaweed.

▲ BLOOMING TASTY

The San Esteban spiny-tailed iguana lives on an arid island in the Mexican Sea of Cortez, and eats cactus flowers and other plant. Iguanas are the main group of leaf-eating lizards, but there may be few leaves in arid habitats, and desert island iguanas often feed on the flowers and fruit of cacti and other water-retaining succulents.

◄ SALTY FOOD

The Galapagos marine iguana is the only truly marine lizard. Although its two Galapagos land iguana relatives have a rich diet of leaves and flowers, the male marine iguana must enter into the cold ocean to feed. Marine iguanas dive down 33 ft to feed on seaweed before returning to bask on the rocks. There is so much salt in their food that they have special glands in their nostrils to get rid of it.

▼ FRUITY FEAST

This little Barbados anole is enjoying a feast of bruised mango fruit. Feeding on fruit is a much easier option than eating leaves. Fruit is easily digested, and it provides much more energy than leaves. However, fruit is seasonal, so lizards that like to eat fruit have to eat other things as well, such as insects.

▲ VEGETARIAN GIANT

Although most monitor lizards are meat-eaters, one species eats fruit more than anything else. Gray's monitor lizard from the Philippines habitually swallows whole fruit and is the world's only plant-eating monitor lizard. It also eats insects, but fruit can make up almost 60 percent of its diet. Other lizards, including the iguanas and chuckwallas of the Americas, eat leaves. Digesting leaves requires a large, specialized gut with valves, to slow down the passage of leaves through the digestive system.

▼ DRIED-OUT DIET

Lizards living in very dry deserts have little green vegetation available to eat. They bulk up their insect diets by feeding on seeds in the dry season when insects are scarce. In the arid Namib Desert of southwestern Africa, the shovel-snouted lizard can survive on wind-blown seeds alone. It obtains not only its energy, but also all of its water requirements from this incredibly dry diet.

Did you know? Some lizards eat insects when young, then move to a diet of leaves as they get older.

Focus on the

The Komodo dragon, or Ora as it is also known, is the largest lizard in the world and the only one believed to include humans in its diet. The size of the dragon has been exaggerated, however—the maximum length for the dragon is not much more than 10 ft—and attacks on humans are very rare. The Komodo dragon is a type of monitor lizard that is confined to four small islands in Indonesia's Komodo group. It has one of the smallest geographical ranges of any of the large carnivores, and is classified as endangered. Komodo dragons feed mainly on large animals, such as deer, which they attack by ambush. Once it is bitten, the prey is doomed to die, even if it escapes. The Komodo dragon's saliva contains deadly bacteria that cause death by blood poisoning within a couple of days.

HUMAN PREY?
This is a view from Baron's Cross on Komodo Island. The Baron's Cross commemorates the Swiss naturalist, Baron Rudolph von Reding, who disappeared on the island in 1974, after he strayed away from his tour group. No one knows for certain how he died, but all that was ever found were his glasses and camera, on the hill where the Baron's Cross now stands.

IN THE TREETOPS
The first thing a newly hatched Komodo dragon does is run for the nearest tree and climb up it quickly. Young Komodo dragons live in the treetops for two years, to be safe from the adults who live on the ground. The young eat large insects, geckos, and skinks.

Komodo Dragon

FIRST TO ARRIVE

Komodo dragons have an extremely good sense of smell and they can detect prey from a long distance. This large adult dragon on Rinca Island has been attracted by the smell of a dead goat. The lizard has powerful jaws, and its muscular legs are armed with talonlike claws, allowing it to rip prey open and devour it very quickly.

THREE'S A CROWD

Two more, slightly smaller, dragons arrive. Soon after this picture was taken, a fight broke out. Eventually, the largest dragon took the goat by the head and started to consume almost the entire carcass, while the other two tore pieces of flesh off. Less than 20 minutes later, the goat had completely disappeared.

ARTIFICIAL GATHERING

In the past, park rangers used to attract Komodo dragons to a feeding station so that tourists could safely watch them. This practice is no longer carried out, since the dragons were becoming reliant on the handouts and were beginning to think of tourists as a source of food. The dragons now act naturally again and look for their own food.

Water for Life

▲ **LAPPING IT UP**
Many lizards drink by lapping up water with their tongues. This Madagascan day gecko has climbed down a tree in order to drink from a puddle. Northern Madagascar, where this day gecko lives, is a very wet region, with regular rainfall. For the majority of lizards, finding water to drink is not a problem.

Like all animals, lizards need water to survive. They obtain it in several ways, depending on the species and habitat. Many drink water from pools and puddles, or get it from dewdrops or condensed fog. Moisture can also be obtained from food. For some lizards, finding water is hard, and a few never drink at all. Lizards living in very dry places produce harder, drier droppings than those in rain forests, where water is plentiful. This helps them conserve water that would otherwise be wasted. Some lizards use water that is produced by their own bodies. "Metabolic" water is created when food is broken down within the body. A few desert-adapted specialists use this "metabolic water" so that they do not need to drink.

▲ **WATERPROOF COAT**
This Bell's dab lizard is basking in the sun. If an amphibian or mammal did this, it would lose a lot of water, either from its moist skin or by sweating, but lizards have tough, dry skin that keeps most water in. This is one reason why reptiles are so common in hot, dry places.

SHADY CHARACTER ▶
The ornate tree lizard lives on large trees along the riverbanks in south-western parts of the U.S.A. These trees have rough bark and broad leaves, which give lots of shade. Rainfall is rare, so the lizard must get all the water it needs from its insect prey. An ornate tree lizard has to eat seven or eight insects a day to get enough water to survive.

Stony Stare of the Basilisk

According to mythology, the basilisk's stare could turn people to stone or cause them to burst into flame. Also known as the Cockatrice or Royal Serpent, this mythological basilisk is shown as a type of dragon, sometimes as a snake-like creature, as in the novel Harry Potter and the Chamber of Secrets. *No one knows what the mythological basilisk looked like because anyone who saw one would never speak again! Real basilisks are harmless Central American lizards whose main claim to fame is that they can run across water.*

▲ DEVIL'S DEW

The thorny devil comes from the deserts of Western Australia, where it hardly ever rains. But the thorny devil's diet of ants does not provide it with enough water to survive. The lizard gets around this problem by drinking any dew that condenses on its body at night. The dew trickles down channels between its "thorns" and into the corner of its mouth.

◄ OUT IN THE SUN

The western brush lizard is closely related to the ornate tree lizard, but it lives in the sparse bushes and trees of the Sonoran Desert. With their small leaves and slender branches, these bushes offer little shade from the sun. The brush lizard loses much more water than the tree lizard, and must eat 11 or 12 insects a day to keep its water levels high enough.

▼ WATER FROM FAT

Some desert geckos, such as Australia's Kimberley fringe-toed velvet gecko, store fat in their tails to help them survive. This fat is mainly used to provide energy when food is short, but it can be broken down to make water. One gram of fat produces just over one gram of water.

39

Body Temperature

A lizard's body temperature depends on the temperature of its surroundings. Unlike birds and mammals, which produce their own body heat, cold-blooded lizards need to bask on hot surfaces such as sun-heated rock, or have warm air around them. In the hot tropics, lizards can be active day or night. Elsewhere, they need the heat of the sun to raise their body temperature. Most lizards speed up this process by basking in the sun, but they must be careful not to get too hot.

▲ ON GUARD

A lizard in the sun has to keep its eyes open for predators. Birds of prey are a particular threat to this African ground agama—the slightest shadow will send it dashing back to its refuge, a hole at the base of the bush. A basking lizard may look like a dozing sunbather, but it is usually alert.

▲ TOO HOT TO HANDLE

If you have ever walked barefoot on sand in the summer, you know how hot it can be. Desert lizards have to face this problem every day. The African ground agama gets around it by standing on the balls of its feet. Other species do a balancing act, standing on two feet with two raised before swapping over.

◄ SUN-POWERED COLOR

Some male lizards adopt very bright colors to attract a female. The male common agama is bright blue and red, but only during the daytime. At night, the sleeping lizard is much drabber and duller, but it quickly becomes more colorful as the day warms up. After a minute or so of basking in the sun, the lizard changes from gray to glowing red and blue again.

▲ BASKING IN THE RAIN FOREST

Not much sunlight reaches the ground in a rain forest, yet some lizards warm up by basking on the rain forest floor. When a rain forest tree falls, it creates a natural gap in the canopy, and a patch of sunlight appears on the ground. In tropical America, ameivas look for these sunny patches, and are usually the first lizards to arrive after a tree has fallen.

▲ WARM AT NIGHT

Lizards that hunt at night still need to be warm to be active. The granite night lizard from California spends the day in a rocky crevice, venturing forth to capture insects and scorpions only after dark. It manages to do this by seeking places where the rocks are still warm from the sun's rays. It is also able to remain active at temperatures too low for most lizards.

CATCHING THE RAYS ▶

So that they can get warm quickly, basking lizards flatten themselves to expose their bodies to the sun or the warm ground. They do this by expanding their ribs outward and making themselves more rounded. Some desert lizards are naturally rounded and can present almost half their body surface to the sun.

ON TIPTOES ▶

This northern desert horned lizard is round and flattened—the ideal shape for basking, since it can present a large surface area to the sun. When it gets too hot, it lifts its underside and tail off the sand. Horned lizards spend long periods of time almost motionless, waiting for the ants that they eat to swarm into reach.

Mating Time

In almost every lizard species, the male courts the female instead of the other way around. Male lizards go to great lengths to attract a mate and often put themselves in danger in the process. Some become bright-colored and others change their behavior, making themselves as obvious to predators as to females. Male lizards may even go without eating, since the urge to mate or defend a female overrides their hunger for food. Males of most lizard species will mate with more than one female if they get the chance. Very few lizards stay with one partner through a mating season, though some Australian shingleback skinks stay together for life. A few lizard species do not need males to reproduce, and females of these species produce offspring without needing to mate.

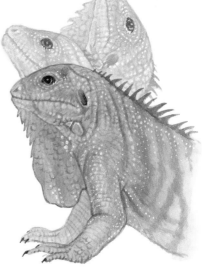

▲ **GREEN NOD**
Male green iguanas use the dewlaps hanging down from their chins to settle disputes about mating territories. The dewlap is green, but dominant males develop a paler-colored head and orange pigment on their shoulders. The dewlap draws attention to the signature bob display.

◀ **WAVING A FLAG**
Anole lizards are well camouflaged from predators, but have a trick that makes them obvious when they want to attract a mate. Anoles possess a bright-colored throat flag, or dewlap, which remains hidden until it is erected for display. Different species have different colored dewlaps, so that males do not attract females of the wrong species.

▲ PUTTING ON A SHOW

In many species of lizard, the males develop bright-colored skin to attract females during the breeding season. The European sand lizard is a good example, since the males sport bright green on the flanks in spring and summer, and the females remain gray-brown.

▼ TEST OF STRENGTH

If a visual display fails to deter a rival, some of the larger lizards, such as these Gould's monitor lizards, will resort to brute force. Fights between male monitors look aggressive as they rear up and try to grapple each other to the ground, but it is rare for either combatant to be injured. Instead, the defeated lizard will break away from the fight and run away.

◄ DANGEROUS LIAISONS

When a male lizard has courted a female and chased away any rivals, he will try to mate with her. In the early stages, he rubs his chin on her neck or nudges her until she lifts her tail and allows him to mate. Some animals, such as these Californian alligator lizards, may mate for a long time, so the female looks out for enemies.

VIRGIN BIRTH ►

Some lizards can produce offspring without mating. When this happens, the babies are identical clones of their mother. Lizards that can give birth without mating include the Indo-Pacific house gecko. Such species are good colonizers of islands, since a single arrival can start a colony all on her own.

Egg Layers

Most lizards lay eggs, but a significant minority, particularly in colder climates, give birth to live young. Although most egg-laying lizards lay eggs with soft, leathery shells, some geckos lay eggs with hard shells like those of birds. Few lizards show interest in their eggs or young, generally leaving after laying or giving birth. Some larger species, however, such as iguanas and monitor lizards, may guard the nest site for a short time after laying. Baby lizards are independent from birth or hatching. As soon as they are born, they face a wide range of predators and few juveniles survive to adulthood.

▲ SPOTTED MOTHER

Leopard geckos inhabit grassland from Iran to India. A female leopard gecko can breed at the age of two and continue to breed for 14 years. Females lay two leathery-shelled eggs one month after mating. A female may produce eight clutches (16 eggs) in a year, and potentially produces over 160 eggs in her life.

◄ BEFORE LAYING

Eggs can be seen in the body of this female house gecko. Most lizards lay eggs rather than give birth to live young. Geckos have clutches of just one or two eggs. Pale areas in the gecko's neck contain a substance called calcium carbonate, which is used to strengthen the eggshell before the eggs are laid.

INDEPENDENT BABY ▶

Hatchling leopard geckos are 3–3½ in long and have a much bolder ringed pattern than adults. During its first few days, the baby survives on its absorbed yolk reserves. When these reserves run out, it starts to hunt for insects.

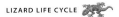

SOFT-SHELLED EGGS ▶
The eggs of most lizards have
soft, leathery shells, and
they are vulnerable to
drying out, so they are
usually laid in moist sand
or soil. Hatching lizards break out
using a small "egg tooth" in the front
of the mouth, which drops off soon
after the lizard has hatched. This newly
emerging collared lizard will survive
for days on the absorbed contents of its
yolk sac before it needs to hunt insects.

◀ MAKING A BREAK FOR IT
Unlike the hard-shelled eggs of most
other geckos, leopard gecko eggs have
leathery shells. After 6–12 weeks the
infant gecko is ready to hatch. It cuts a
small hole in the eggshell using a small
egg tooth on the front of its jaw. Once it
has absorbed the last of the yolk from its
yolk sac and learned to breathe using its
lungs, it breaks out of the shell.

Did you know? A baby lizard's egg tooth drops off soon after it has slit a hole in the egg and hatched.

HARD PROTECTION ▶
Tree-living geckos, such as the gold dust day gecko,
lay just one pair of eggs. The moment they are laid,
they are soft and can fit into crevices in bark or on
walls, sticking to both surfaces and the other egg. The eggs
harden quickly when they come into contact with the air,
giving the developing babies protection from drying out.

Birth and Hatching

Some species of lizards lay eggs and others give birth to live young. Female lizards who give birth carry their offspring for less time than a female who lays eggs. Most lizards in warm climates lay eggs, but those living in colder habitats, such as Scandinavia, Patagonia, and Tasmania, usually give birth to live young. Such females can protect their young. They can seek out the sun and avoid enemies until the babies are ready to be born. When they are born, the mother rarely takes care of them. Whether they are born or hatch from eggs, the juvenile lizards exist for a while on nutrients absorbed from the yolk sac, but they must soon become predators of insects and other small animals, or they will be eaten by larger creatures than themselves.

▲ LIVE YOUNG

About one in five lizard species give birth to live young. The babies are born wrapped in thin, transparent sacs, from which they soon escape, taking a first breath in the process. Many live-bearing lizards live where it would be too cold for eggs to incubate. The common lizard has live young and lives as far north as Scandinavia inside the Arctic Circle.

◀ PROTECTIVE MOTHER

Only one lizard guards its young, the Solomons monkey-tail skink. Females usually give birth to a single infant, which never strays far from its mother and seeks shelter underneath her if it is threatened. Since the skink is a plant-eater, it is important that the baby eats some of its mother's droppings to get the microbes needed for it to digest leaves.

▲ GIVING BIRTH

Adult common lizards mate from March to June, depending on their location. The embryos take up to three months to develop inside the female, and she gives birth to a single litter between July and September. The average size of a litter is seven or eight, but large females may give birth to up to 11 offspring. The babies are born in a membranous sac, from which they escape within seconds. In warmer parts of the world, the common lizard may lay eggs. All baby common lizards have an egg tooth, even those that are born rather than laid in eggs.

Beware of Lizards
Iguanas might look cute when they are small, but these little green lizards can grow to six feet in length. All iguanas need to have special lighting and follow a special diet if they are to keep healthy. When they are three years old, male green iguanas may become quite aggressive in the breeding season, biting and using the tail as a whip. Female iguanas often become eggbound in captivity because they have not been allowed to mate and lay eggs. An eggbound lizard may die. You should never buy a lizard on impulse or because it looks cute. Even baby Komodo dragons look cute—but they have a nasty bite.

Did you know? Green iguanas guard their eggs to stop others digging them up and laying their own.

▲ FAST WARM UP

Baby common lizards are just under 1½ in long. They are independent from birth, and must find their own food and avoid numerous predators if they are to survive to adulthood. In Britain, newborn common lizards are much darker than adults. They may even be black, a color that helps them warm up faster in the sun, in order to hunt and be alert enough to avoid getting captured.

Lizards Under Attack

Snakes, birds of prey, and mammals, such as mongooses and meerkats, are all enemies of lizards, and they are capable of catching even the most alert, fast-moving species by day and night. More unusual predators include other lizards and various large invertebrates, including spiders, scorpions, and centipedes. Many predators are opportunistic and include lizards as only part of their diet. But others are more specialized and regularly prey on them—snakes in particular. Lizards have evolved all sorts of ways of escaping from predators, but the main reason that they survive as species is that they are simply so abundant. A single lizard can have dozens of offspring in a lifetime, and only a few of those offspring have to survive long enough to breed for the species to continue.

▲ STRENGTH IN NUMBERS
A single army ant would be a small snack for most lizards, but a swarm of army ants is another story. These fierce insects march across the rain forest floor in South America and overpower anything that gets in their way. Most of their prey is made up of other insects, but sometimes they kill and eat small lizards, too.

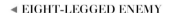

◄ EIGHT-LEGGED ENEMY
Invertebrates are animals without a backbone. Many species of lizards feed on invertebrates, but sometimes large invertebrates turn the tables and make the lizards their prey. In many parts of the world, arachnids, such as scorpions and large spiders, hunt and kill small lizards. This wheel spider is eating a web-footed gecko that it has caught along the dunes of southwest Africa's Namib desert.

48

◄ EATING EACH OTHER

A few lizards specialize in eating other lizards. For example, the slender pygopodid snake-lizards are specialist predators of skinks. In the deserts of North America, small spiny lizards are the main prey of larger lizard species. Here a black-collared lizard has caught a spiny lizard that was basking among the rocks.

CAUGHT UP IN THE COILS ►

A huge number of snakes prey on lizards and some feed on very little else. The common Asian wolf snake is one species that specializes in hunting lizards. Active at night, often inside houses, it will search underneath baskets, boxes, and boards for small lizards, which are then grabbed and constricted before they are eaten. This wolf snake has a house gecko in its coils.

◄ DEATH FROM ABOVE

A few birds, such as secretary birds and the kookaburra, specialize in killing and eating snakes and lizards. Many other birds, including this black-shouldered kite from Namibia, will eat any basking lizard that is not paying attention to the threat from the skies. Small lizards are swallowed head first and whole, and larger ones are torn apart by beak and claw to be eaten in chunks.

STRAIGHT FOR THE HEAD ►

The reptile-eating habits of some mammals are well known. Meerkats are small members of the same family as the cobra-killing mongooses. Smaller than a mongoose, the meerkat feeds on roots and small animals, including lizards. The meerkat's long canine teeth makes eating lizards easy, especially since the head is targeted first.

Defense Methods

Many lizards are small and looked upon as food by other animals. To escape being eaten, lizards have evolved a wide array of defensive mechanisms. One of the most effective is simply being well camouflaged and staying still to avoid detection. When this fails, the lizard may have to adopt a more active method of defending itself. Running away, diving off a branch, or even gliding to freedom are all simple escape procedures. But many lizards have evolved more elaborate defensive behavior, including displays intended to intimidate or confuse potential predators. Some of these are among the most extreme seen anywhere in the animal kingdom.

▲ BOLD DEFENSE

The toad-headed agama of Iran and southern Russia puts on a bold defense display. When it is threatened, it raises its front, opens its mouth wide, and extends flaps at both sides to make it look threatening. It then hisses, waves its tail like a scorpion, and jumps toward its enemy.

◄ PUTTING ON A SHOW

The Australian frilled lizard's first reaction to danger is to open its mouth wide to spread its neck frill. All of this makes the lizard seem suddenly less like an easy meal and more like a large, dangerous opponent. If this display fails to scare a predator, the lizard turns tail and runs, the frill trailing around its neck like a partially closed umbrella. The frilled lizard uses its display to scare rivals as well as predators.

THREATENING DISPLAY ▶

The shingleback skink from Australia tries to frighten predators by opening its mouth and sticking out its bright blue tongue. These lizards have short legs so they cannot run away, and must stand their ground. The rolling tongue, combined with a flattening and curving of the body, and a hiss, is enough to intimidate most animals.

▲ SEEING RED

The horned lizards of Mexico and the U.S.A. have one of the strangest defense mechanisms of any animal—they squirt foul-tasting blood from the corners of their eyes. They use this defense only against large predators. Birds and rodents are usually chased away by the lizard's prickly spines.

▼ FIGHTING TINY ENEMIES

New Guinea's green-blooded skinks have a pigment in their blood that makes it bright green. This is thought to be a defense against the tiny blood parasites that cause a disease called malaria. Lizards suffer from seven types of malaria. The skinks' blood is believed to be so toxic, the malarial parasite cannot survive.

▼ CHAMPION WRESTLER

Monitor lizards have powerful jaws, which can deliver a painful bite. They use their tails as whips, dealing rapid blows to their enemies. When the argus monitor is threatened, it makes itself look bigger by standing on its hind feet and inflating its throat. If this fails, it attacks, wrestling fiercely until its opponent flees.

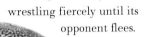

Did you know? The frilled lizard can run on its back legs at speeds of more than 12½ m.p.h.

Color and Camouflage

A lizard's color is usually dictated by the habitat in which it lives: most desert lizards are sandy brown, most tree-living species are bark-colored or green. By matching themselves to the color of their background, they become well camouflaged, which protects them from animals that want to eat them. Some lizards take camouflage one step further and actually look like objects from their surroundings. Color is also important socially. Many male lizards adopt bright colors in the mating season, or change color or expose bright parts of the body when confronted by a rival.

▲ DEAD LEAF
Not all chameleons are green or camouflaged like living leaves. The West African pygmy chameleon lives in low vegetation in forests and is a drab brown with a series of darker lines making it look like a dead leaf. When the pygmy chameleon feels threatened, it just falls to the forest floor and lies still, disappearing among the leaf litter.

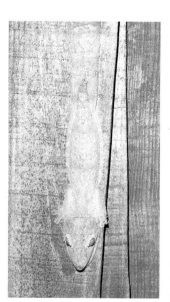

◄ WOODEN PERFORMANCE ►
Chameleons are not the only lizards capable of changing their pattern or color. The Malagasy flat-tailed gecko can also alter its appearance, shown here as it matches the wooden planks of a hut (left) and the bark of a tree (right). By combining camouflage with a flattened body edged with thin fringes of skin, this nocturnal gecko can sleep unseen during the day. Its gripping toes mean that it can merge into the background on vertical surfaces or even the undersides of branches. At night, it wakes up again to feed.

▲ LEGS LIKE STICKS

The Sri Lankan kangaroo lizard has legs
that look like fine twigs, and body and
head patterns that look like a dead leaf or
fern frond. When a predator approaches,
the kangaroo lizard skips quickly across
the forest floor and then disappears into
the dead leaves. It is often found near
forest streams, and can run across water.

Omen of Evil

*Chameleons are
considered evil omens
in Africa, but nowhere
are they feared as
much as on the island
of Madagascar, where
the giant panther
chameleon is avoided
at all costs. Drivers
who would not think
twice about hitting a dog or a chicken swerve to
avoid chameleons, preferring to risk a serious
accident rather than incur the wrath of an angry
spirit. Chameleons are also believed by some
Malagasy people to be poisonous, so they are never
handled or eaten, even when other meat is scarce.*

◄ SPOTLIT SIDES

In 1938, a British naturalist captured a small, cave-dwelling
lizard in Trinidad and reported that it had white spots on
its flanks that glowed like a ship's portholes. Recently, a
male lizard was caught, and the 1938 report was
proved correct. The purpose of the spots is
unknown, but it is thought they might
be used to startle predators.

STANDING OUT ►

Four-fingered skinks are usually brown
and blend in with the leaf litter, but this
individual is an albino. Being born an
albino can make life more dangerous.
Albinos lack colored pigment and stand
out from their surroundings, making
them easy targets for predators. Not only
are they more likely to be eaten, they are
also thought to be vulnerable to sunburn.

Focus on

The beaded lizard and the Gila monster are the world's only venomous lizards. They are found from southwestern U.S.A. through western Mexico to Guatemala in Central America. Both feed on eggs, fledgling birds and newborn rodents, such as rats and mice. Since they do not need venom to deal with such harmless prey, the lizards' poison is mainly for defense. They hang on when they bite, forcing more venom into the wound. The poison causes great pain, but there are no records of people being killed by these lizards.

RIVER MONSTER

Named after the Gila River, where it was first encountered by settlers, the Gila monster is a spectacular lizard. Its rounded head is covered in large, studlike scales a little larger than those on its body. Bulges in the rear of the powerful lower jaw indicate the position of the bulbous venom glands.

NO RELATION

It was once thought the Gila monster and beaded lizard might be related to snakes. But the snake has its venom glands and fangs in the upper jaw, while the lizard's venom teeth are in the lower jaw of its skull. This means venom has evolved in these lizards separately from its evolution in snakes.

BEADED BEAST

When it is seen close up, the beaded lizard is easily distinguished from its northern relative. It is less colorful than the Gila monster, and its yellow and brown skin camouflage it well. Its head is longer and more squarish, and the neck is longer. The beaded lizard, so called because of its beadlike scales, is larger but less aggressive than the Gila monster.

Venomous Lizards

VENOMOUS WARNING
When it feels threatened, the Gila monster opens its mouth like a large blue-tongue skink. But the Gila monster has more to back up its threat than most lizards. Its bite is not only painful, but can result in a venomous bite bad enough to require urgent medical attention.

DESERT DWELLER
The Gila monster is most at home in saguero cactus desert. Its bright pink and black warning colors send out a clear message to potential predators, "Mess with me at your own risk." It may look sluggish, but the Gila monster can move remarkably quickly.

WHERE DO THEY LIVE?
Found in the southwestern U.S.A. and northwest Mexico, from Utah to north Sinaloa, the Gila monster spends much of its life underground, hunting in rodent burrows. It is rarely seen except at dusk or after nightfall.

AT HOME IN THE WOODS
The beaded lizard lives in woodland and scrub in Guatemala, west Mexico and south Sonora. With a longer neck, tail and legs than the Gila monster, it can reach almost 3 ft. Although it is in the main a ground-dweller, it can climb trees.

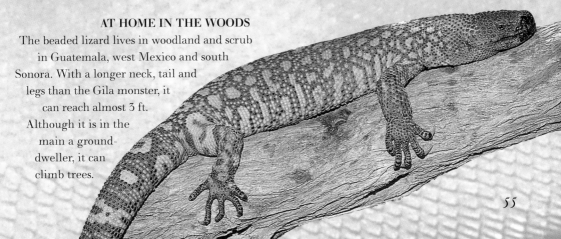

Watching Lizards

There are many more lizards in the tropics than in other parts of the world, but lizard watching can be carried out anywhere there are lizards. When watching lizards, you are likely to see more if you move slowly and quietly, and stop often to look around. Avoid casting a shadow ahead of you, and try to wear drab clothes, because some lizards have color vision. The best time to see lizards in temperate countries is in the early morning when they come out to bask and are slightly less alert. In the tropics, you can find lizards everywhere, and at all times of day and night. If you really enjoy lizard watching, you might like to go to college and become an herpetologist (a scientist who studies reptiles).

▲ CAUGHT ON CAMERA
Photography is a very satisfying way to record the lizards you find, although not all lizards are as large and impressive as this Komodo dragon, which the author is photographing. A macro lens and a flash gun help capture all the detail in small lizards.

▲ QUIET CONTEMPLATION
Observations from a short distance away must be made without disturbing the lizards. Approach very quietly and slowly, and avoid casting your shadow across them, like this herpetologist who is watching sand lizards in Dorset, England.

KEEPING WATCH ▶
Lizards are very common in the tropics, and they can be found in many places. These two herpetologists are searching for green-blooded skinks high on Mount Wilhelm, the tallest mountain in Papua New Guinea. Binoculars help you scan branches for small species, but you will still have to look very hard and be able to identify what you are looking at when you find it.

SPOTTERS' GUIDE ▶

Lizards include many different families, and a lizard watcher must learn how to identify them. A knowledge of head shape, size of scales, and so on is often helpful. Closely related species may look very similar, but looking at markings and counting the number of the scales on the head helps make an accurate identification.

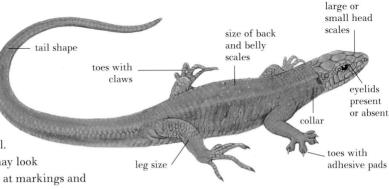

tail shape

toes with claws

size of back and belly scales

large or small head scales

eyelids present or absent

collar

toes with adhesive pads

leg size

This drawing shows features from several lizards

◀ IN THE FIELD

The ultimate lizard watching must be performing fieldwork in the tropics. Working in a reserve studying all the lizards found there is very satisfying. This sort of fieldwork requires good background knowledge and equipment, such as a microscope, to examine scales in order to identify species. Herpetologists often discover new species when working in remote parts of the world.

▼ HOW TO HOLD LIZARDS

When you hold lizards, it is important to support them so that they cannot fall or injure themselves trying to escape. Lizards can bite and scratch. This young green iguana is being held so that it cannot bite, and its legs are secured beside its body. You should never grab a lizard by its tail.

Great Gecko
There is just one Delcourt's giant gecko at the Natural History Museum in Marseilles in France. Collected some time between 1833 and 1869, it went unnoticed until 1979 when experts examined it and found it was a new species. More than 2 ft. long, it is twice the size of any other gecko. No one is sure where it came from, but it may have come from New Zealand.

Human Threats

Wild lizards are threatened by humans in many varied ways. People collect and kill them for their meat, their skins, their eggs, and their internal organs. They are also caught to be sold as pets, particularly the rarer and more exotic species. Many lizards are killed out of fear—chameleons and geckos are considered devils by some native peoples, for instance. Many lizards die simply because they make the mistake of looking for insects on a busy road. Less obvious threats include habitat destruction and the introduction of new predators, such as cats and rats. Island lizard species are particularly vulnerable to introduced predators, since they usually have only small populations and may be found nowhere else. Other introduced animals, such as goats, may destroy lizards' habitats, leaving them with nowhere to live.

▲ **KILLED FOR FASHION**
This monitor lizard skin was found by the author when he joined a police raid on a large illegal factory in Asia, in which wild reptiles are killed and skinned in huge numbers. Lizard-skin handbags, shoes, belts, and coats are still popular fashion items. The police found bags of skins from monitor lizards and pythons, and rescued and released live reptiles.

◄ **CAUGHT FOR THE POT**
Tribal rain forest people have always eaten reptiles and other animals. Such small-scale hunting does no real damage, but when hunters start supplying markets in the towns, it becomes a serious problem. These green iguanas are alive but in shock. Keeping them alive means that their meat stays fresh for the customer.

▲ GORY SOUVENIRS

Although endangered species are protected by international laws, in some countries they can still be found for sale to tourists. This shop is selling stuffed monitor lizards, pythons, and cobras, reptiles that are all becoming very rare in the wild. Buying this type of souvenir may lead to the buyer being prosecuted when they return to their own country.

▲ HABITAT DESTRUCTION

Tropical rain forests have been shrinking for many years due to "slash and burn" farming and clearance of trees for timber. The result is huge loss of habitat and the disappearance of many forest species.

▼ TERRIBLE CONSEQUENCES

Introducing destructive animals to a new place can have catastrophic results. When the brown tree snake was introduced to the island of Guam, it began eating the native geckos, skinks, and flightless birds. Now the lizards are very rare and most of the flightless birds have become extinct.

▲ DANGER ON THE ROAD

Lizards cross roads to hunt, find mates, or move to new areas. Many, such as this Namibian flapneck chameleon, are too slow to get out of the way of cars. The death toll in some areas is huge. Near many busy towns, wildlife has been almost wiped out.

Conservation

Individual species can be protected and so can habitats. Conservation means all the ways there are of protecting and taking care of wildlife for the future. Breeding endangered species in captivity is an important part of conservation, as is the education of people in places where animals are threatened. The education of young people is very important, because one day they will be the decision-makers with the power to decide what happens to threatened species. Conservation also involves fighting against illegal trade and the smuggling of animal skins, meat, and live reptiles for the pet trade.

▲ TAKING CARE OF THE LAND

There is no point in protecting a species if the habitat in which it lives is not also protected. Unique habitats such as this heathland often contain species found nowhere else. If the habitat is threatened, the species may become extinct. Many habitats are destroyed and their species lost before anything has been done to save them.

▼ CAPTIVE BREEDING

One way to help endangered species is to breed them in captivity. The monkey-tail skink was threatened in its native Solomon Islands, so zoos in the U.S.A. and Europe began breeding them in captivity. Researchers have learned a lot about these lizards, and the unusual maternal behavior of the females. Populations built up in projects like this can be used to provide animals for reintroduction into the wild in the future.

▲ PROTECTIVE PENS

Conservation usually involves fieldwork. Biologists on Komodo are monitoring the hatching of baby Komodo dragons. They must catch all the hatchlings just after they emerge from the nest. The metal screening around the nest protects the dragons.

CENTER FOR LEARNING ▶
Education is an important part of
conservation. If people do not know
about animals, they are less likely to
care if they become extinct. Education
helps people to see how interesting their
local wildlife is. This center in England
tells people about British reptiles.
Wildlife can also be valuable—Komodo
islanders earn their livings from tourists
who come to see the dragons.

◀ KEEPING TRACK
Baby Komodo dragons have been
captured and are being weighed inside
a little cage. A few of them will be
fitted with radio-tracking devices so
that researchers can follow their daily
activity in the forest once they have been
released. The dragons spend the first
two years of life in
the trees and
without
transmitters it
would be
impossible to
find them, let
alone follow them.

Did you know? The sand lizard is Britain's rarest lizard. Destruction of habitat threatens its survival!

DRIFT FENCE ▶
Many lizards live in leaf-litter
and the top layers of soil. Drift
fences are used to capture
burrowing lizards. They come
to the surface at night after
rain and bump into the fence.
Then they travel along it
and fall into buckets buried
along its length. By looking at
what ends up in the buckets,
scientists can find out which
species live on the forest floor.

GLOSSARY

Albino
An animal that lacks color on all or part of its body, and that belongs to a species that is usually colored.

Amphisbaenian
A legless reptile that has evolved from the lizards.

Arid
Very dry.

Bask
To lie in the warmth of the sun.

Bifurcated tail
A V-shaped tail that is formed when one tail does not fully come off and a second tail then grows from the wound.

Bird of prey
A predatory bird with sharp claws and a hooked beak, such as an eagle or falcon, that hunts animals.

Camouflage
Colors and patterns that help an animal blend into its surroundings.

Carrion
Animals that have been dead for some time.

Carnivore
An animal that eats only meat or fish.

Clutch
The number of eggs laid by a female at one time.

Cold-blooded
An animal that maintains its body temperature at the same level as, or higher than, its surroundings by basking or sheltering, and does not produce its own body heat.

Colony
A large group of animals of the same species that live together.

Crustacean
A type of invertebrate such as crabs, slaters, and woodlice.

Dewlap
A flap of skin under the chin, often brightly colored and used for display.

Digestion
The process by which food is broken down so that it can be absorbed into the body.

Eardrum
Part of the ear that vibrates when sound hits it.

Egg tooth
A small tooth in the front of a baby lizard's mouth, which it uses to slit open the egg.

Endangered
A species that is at risk of becoming extinct.

Epidermis
The outer layer of the skin.

Evolution
The process by which living things adapt over generations to changes in their surroundings.

Extinct
When every member of a species of animal or plant is dead.

Gallbladder
A small organ attached to the liver.

Habitat
The type of place where an animal naturally lives.

Hard-tongued lizards
All lizards not contained in the group Iguania.

Herbivore
An animal that eats only plants.

Hibernation
A long period of inactivity when all body processes are slowed down in very cold weather.

Iguania
The name given to the group of lizards containing iguanas, agamas, chameleons, anoles, swift lizards, lava lizards, basilisks, and spiny lizards.

Incubation
Using heat to help eggs develop.

Intestine
Part of an animal's digestive system.

Invertebrate
An animal without a backbone.

Jacobson's organ
A sensitive organ in the roof of the mouth into which the tongue places scent particles.

Keratin
A horny substance that makes up a lizard's scales.

Mammal
An animal with fur or hair and a backbone, which can control its own body temperature. All female mammals feed their young on milk.

Marine
Sea-living or seagoing.

Membrane
A thin film, skin, or layer.

Microbes
Living things, such as bacteria too small to be seen with the naked eye.

Omnivore
An animal that eats plants and meat.

Osteoderms
Rigid plates that add strength to a lizard's skin.

Parasite
A living thing that lives on or inside another living thing and does not benefit its host.

Pigment
Colored matter in the skin.

Predator
An animal that hunts and kills other animals for food.

Prehensile
Able to grip.

Prehistoric
Dating from long ago, before people wrote down historical records.

Prey
An animal that is hunted and eaten by other animals.

Pupil
The dark opening in the middle of the eye that allows light to enter.

Reptile
A scaly, cold-blooded animal with a backbone. Reptiles include lizards, snakes, crocodilians, and turtles.

Rodent
An animal such as a rat, mouse, or squirrel with chisel-shaped incisors (front teeth) used for gnawing.

Scavenger
An animal that feeds on carrion.

Scutes
The thick, sometimes bony, scales that cover the bodies of some lizards.

Slash and burn
Cutting down and burning forests to create farmland.

Sloughing
Shedding skin. Lizards slough when a new layer of epidermis has grown underneath the old skin.

Species
A group of animals that share the same characteristics and can breed with one another to produce fertile young.

Succulent
A plant that stores water in its stem or leaves.

Territory
An area of land that one or more animals defend against members of the same species and other species.

Tropics
The hot regions or countries near the Equator and between the Tropic of Cancer and the Tropic of Capricorn.

Tuataras
Lizardlike animals that have their own separate reptile group. Today there are only two living species in New Zealand.

Venom
Poisonous fluid produced by two lizards, the Gila monster and the beaded lizard, for defense from predators.

Vertebrate
An animal with a backbone.

Viviparous
Gives birth to live young, instead of laying eggs.

Warm-blooded
An animal that can maintain its body temperature at the same level all the time.

Yolk
Food material that is rich in protein and fats, which nourishes an embryo inside an egg.

Picture Acknowledgements

l = left, r = right, m = middle
t = top, b = bottom

Art Archive/Dagli Orti: 39tl; Aaron Bauer: 57br; Chris Brown: 41tr; Corbis: 48b; Ecoscene: 18t, 49cr; Bill Love: 5b; Chris Mattison: 10bl, 13bl, 16t, 18br, 19br, 25cl, 29b, 42, 44bl, 45b, 46t, 47t, 49cl; Natural History Museum: 4b; NHPA: 1, 2t, 2b, 4t, 4c, 7t, 8t, 9cr, 9b, 10t, 11c, 11b, 13tl, 16bl, 17b, 18bl, 19t, 20l, 23t, 23br, 25cr, 28c, 28b, 29tl, 29tr, 31tr, 31c, 32b, 33tl, 33c, 33b, 35tr, 35b, 37b, 38bl, 39tr, 40t, 41b, 43tl, 43tr, 43bl, 45t, 45c, 48t, 49t, 49b, 50t, 52br, 53tr, 55tr, 55c, 60t, 62, 63b; Nature Picture Library: 38t, 51tl; Papilio: 5t, 9cl, 24t; RSPCA: 59tl, 59br, 61t; Science Photo Library: 6t, 19bl, 34b; John Sullivan/Ribbit Photography: 6b, 39bl; Jane Burton/Warren Photographic: 35tl; Kim Taylor/Warren Photographic: 2c, 3, 6c, 12t, 30, 40c, 47tr, 51tr.

All other photographs supplied courtesy of the author.

INDEX